there is no such thing as luck

by colleen barry

Cover Designer: Colleen Barry

Editor: Katie Smith

Other Contributors: Theresa Nadolny, Richard Nadolny, Mike Barry, Diane Barry

ISBN-10: 1511692995

ISBN-13: 978-1511692991

LCCN:

CreateSpace Independent Publishing Platform

North Charleston, SC

Visit ThereIsNoSuchThingAsLuck.com to download the worksheets in this book for kindle or audio versions, or for use in future growth endeavors.

table of contents

forward & acknowledgements

This book is the product of two years of extensive learning that I affectionately call "My Library Card MBA." I have read dozens of books and articles about business, goal-setting, entrepreneurship, personal growth, psychology, management, and coaching. Several common themes emerged — heck, they nearly slapped me across the face and demanded to be heard! In every book and in every case study, regardless of the fields in which the subjects applied themselves, success was the result of a good plan and consistent effort.

The concepts in this book are derived from and inspired by the writings of the following thought-leaders (in alphabetical order): Shawn Achor, Jon Acuff, David Allen, Colleen Barrett, Jonah Berger, Ken Blanchard, Bob Burg, Jack Canfield, Jim Collins, Jack Cotton, Jeremy Donovan, Peter Drucker, Carol Dweck, T. Harv Ecker, Hal Elrod, Michael Gerber, Malcolm Gladwell, Jon Gordon, Warren Greshes, Napoleon Hill, Tony Hseih, Walter Isaacson, Spencer Johnson, Josh Kaufman, Dave Logan, Michael Maher, Og Mandino, Ivan Misner, Dan Pink, Robert Pirsig, Tony Robbins, David Rock,

Seth Rodin, Jim Rohn, Keith Rosen, Gretchen Rubin, Sheryl Sandberg, Lewis Schiff, Simon Sinek, Thomas Stanley, Brian Tracy, Jack Trout, and others.

I want to thank several people. First, my bosses and friends, Larry Rideout and Paul McGann. They showed tremendous faith in me when they led me to this exciting new career — it is the most rewarding job I have ever had. The conversation went something like this, over a nice lunch in the Back Bay neighborhood of Boston:

> Paul: "What would you think about being a Business Coach for our agents?"
> Me: "I have never done anything like that before. I wouldn't even know where to begin."
> Larry: "Great! How soon can you start?"

They have the most talented, hard working, and passionate team in the country (I might be biased). It is an honor to work with them every day.

I also want to thank the following people: My mom and dad — Theresa Nadolny and Mike Barry — (and their spouses, Richard and Diane) who have been very supportive and have always believed in me. They have given the best advice, and only when I needed it. My siblings — Ray, Kyle, and Chelsea — who inspire me every day with their intelligence, kindness, and humor. My friends who are brilliant, creative, and have the guts to try new things — you know who you are. My son, Albert, for making crystal clear everything I have ever wanted in this life. You make me want to become the mom you deserve.

Lastly, I ~~want~~ need to thank my wife, Katie, who has never once doubted me or my cockamamie ideas. She says she thinks I am almost as smart as her brother, the all-knowing and incredibly gifted musician, Dave "Smoota" Smith... I am *almost* as smart as he! That has, in part, driven me to try to be worthy of her belief in me. I intend for that to be a life-long goal.

shallow (wo)men believe in luck.
strong (wo)men believe in
cause and effect.
- ralph waldo emerson

introduction

Luck is a myth. It is an artificial concept that removes from our hands the power to create success. We are led to believe that opportunity appears only for a blessed few — those upon whom shines a special light.

That is a lie.

What is luck? It is merely opportunity that has been recognized and grasped. Success is intentional. Opportunity is abundant. We only need to train our minds to look for it; then train ourselves to grasp it. And, when we do, success is more than intentional; it is inevitable.

you are either
the driver in your success
or the passenger in your failure.

- me

Most of the examples in this book are related to the real estate industry. It is only because that is the nature of my job. But, the concepts herein are equally as effective in other areas of interest. Real estate was the focus of only a few of the dozens of books, classes, and seminars that are my inspiration for this book. The mindset and methods that drive success in any field are the same.

Let's begin...

the voyage of discovery
is not in seeking new landscapes
but in having new eyes.

- marcel proust

let's get started

I describe six steps in this book. They will help you find more opportunity than ever before. I think of the following as "Six Steps to Making Your Own Luck:"

1. set goals
2. study hard
3. seek need
4. share expertise
5. step up
6. say thanks

Be sure to complete each step. Skipping even one step will reduce the number of opportunities available to you. These are not complicated or difficult. You are more than capable.

Mastering these steps requires practice and commitment. If you are reading this book, some part of you wants to achieve more. Whether you want to improve your current position in business or change careers entirely, you owe it to yourself to try.

1. set goals
2. study hard
3. seek need
4. share expertise
5. step up
6. say thanks

setting goals
is the first step
in turning the invisible
into the visible.
- tony robbins

1. set goals

An opportunity is simply a chance to achieve all or part of a goal. In order to recognize opportunity when it comes, you must first know the goal it needs to serve. In other words, think of your goal as a destination on a map, and each opportunity as a street that helps you get there.

Once you have identified your goals, you will need to look for opportunities that...

- get you closer to your goals
- allow you to practice the skills that are needed to achieve your goals
- position you as an expert in your field
- introduce you to people who can help you achieve your goals
- introduce you to people who *know* people who can help you achieve your goals

Let's learn how to set goals. Begin by thinking about what you want your business or career to look like. My favorite way to do this is to have you imagine yourself one year from now, celebrating success. Imagine the excitement and sense of accomplishment you feel. Now answer these questions:

- What did I accomplish to get here?
- Who helped me to get here?
- What activities led to my success?
- Which of my experiences and skills convinced someone to give me an opportunity?

Next, you will compose your goals on paper. That is one way to better ensure that you will accomplish your goals. A study conducted at the Dominican University of California showed that writing down goals increased the likelihood that they would be achieved by 42 percent.[1] That is what I call a meaningful difference!

Now, you want *the way* you have written your goals to also assure your success. One proven method for creating achievable goals is to make them S.M.A.R.T.

Specific
Measurable
Attainable
Relevant
Time-bound

This concept is often attributed to Peter Drucker's 1954 book, "The Practice of Management." Being S.M.A.R.T. forces us to be specific — this is necessary if we are to recognize all relevant opportunities.

For example, a typical, non-S.M.A.R.T. goal for a real estate agent might be: *I want to sell more homes.* This is far too vague. It does not identify how we will achieve the goal, what actions we need to take, or when we need to take action to work toward our goal.

An example of a S.M.A.R.T. goal is: *I will list ten homes this year by reaching out to 1,000 home owners by mail each month.* This tells us what we need to do and when we need to do it. It also allows us to cross the task off of our list every month with a sense of accomplishment. That feeling of accomplishment, along with the inevitable results, will keep us motivated.

How did I select a quantity of 1,000 home owners? I know from basic research that direct mail campaigns (if sufficiently repeated) will yield a four percent rate of response[2]. I also know from talking to real estate agents that only some of the responses will yield an appointment, and fewer still will turn into a listing (for the purposes of this example, let's say 25%). So, four percent of 1,000 is 40 appointments. 25% of 40 appointments is 10 listings. I am making an educated guess that this level of effort will get us to 10 new listings.

Let's try another. A non-S.M.A.R.T. goal for a budding writer might be: *I want to write my first book.* This doesn't tell us when or how. In fact, the size of the goal is intimidating enough to prevent even the most skilled writer from taking the first step.

An example of a S.M.A.R.T. goal for this writer is: *I will write my first book in six months by first writing an outline, then completing one chapter each week.*

Brian Tracy, author of "Goals!" said, "People with clear, written goals accomplish far more in a shorter period of time than people without them could ever imagine." I know this works. It is how I earned my job title. It is how I started publishing articles. It is how I am writing this book.

exercise one

For our first exercise, identify and write down three S.M.A.R.T.
goals. Do not write anything in the space next to #4. Post this sheet
where you will see it every day.

1. _____

_____

_____

_____

2. _____

_____

_____

_____

3. _____

_____

_____

_____

4. ....

....

....

....

1. set goals
2. **study hard**
3. seek need
4. share expertise
5. step up
6. say thanks

opportunity favors
the prepared mind.
- louis pasteur

2. study hard

Now that you have identified your three goals, you can decide
which new knowledge or skills you might need to achieve them. If
you don't need new knowledge or skills, you can identify the
existing skills that should be polished. This will require dedication
and time.

In Og Mandino's brief and poetic book, "The Greatest Salesman in
the World," the following mantra appears: "Today I will multiply my
value a hundredfold." Not only is this entirely possible, but it is also
the only way to create success stories. Every book and case study
that I have read has told story after story of success won through
intentional professional growth.

Carol Dweck's "Mindset" dispels the myths of talent. Talent can be
born with us, but it is also grown through intentional effort. I
remember hearing a concert pianist telling a story about meeting a
woman at a dinner party. She said to him, "I would give anything to
have your ability." His response: "No, you wouldn't." While the
sharpness of his response likely stung her, the content of it was true.
He spent countless hours every day of his life to develop his ability.

He wasn't born playing Chopin; it took incredible dedication. If that woman were honestly willing to give anything, she would have given the required time and effort to achieve piano virtuosity. What we are talking about in this book won't require but a small percentage of what is required to play Chopin at Symphony Hall. It is achievable.

Many people tell me that they don't have the time to do this. But, they are usually wrong. If you are a television watcher, keep track of the hours you spend watching TV. You might decide it is time to unplug it or take the batteries out of the remote control. Or you may need to get up an hour earlier every day. Perhaps you can use your commuting time to read books on the train or listen to books as you drive to and from work. You can become an expert by applying an hour or two per day toward learning — just an hour or two.

In Jack Canfield's brilliant book, "The Success Principles," he shares this principle: "Learn More to Earn More." Mr. Canfield has read over 3,000 books in his effort to be the best he can be. You don't need to read 3,000 books. Instead, start by brainstorming the types of resources you can use to grow — books, classes, videos, or other ways of acquiring skill and knowledge. Then voraciously devour them. You will feel your mind expanding with every new bit of knowledge. Then, find mentors who have achieved success in this field. Learn from them at every opportunity and thank them for their time and generosity.

Let's call this your "bonus goal." Goal number four should sound like this: *I will become an expert in (chosen topic) by reading (commit to a number) books each month*. In a few moments, you will add this new goal to your goals page (exercise 1).

Here's an example: If you were a real estate agent who wanted to sell more luxury homes in the Cambridge neighborhood of Greater Boston, you would need to become an expert in the market trends of that area — what has sold, what is available, how fast homes sell, average price points, and year-over-year changes. You would also need to attend every open house in the luxury market. You are not likely to be hired unless you have first-hand knowledge of these homes. This research should be updated weekly, if not daily.

This is another example: If you were an actor who wanted to be cast in local plays, you would need to learn the plays that are favored by local theaters and directors. Learn about the playwrights, the meaning of the plays, and when they have been produced in the past. You might focus on one new play every month. That would be twelve plays in one year!

To attract a new audience and build true confidence, you need to learn that audience's wants, needs, and concerns. Then you must become an expert in providing solutions.

There is research to be done and knowledge to be gained. If you try to skip this step, you will not be prepared for the opportunity when it arrives — or worse, you might damage your reputation by bungling it! This effort is the secret side of luck. Most overnight successes were years in the making; years of dedicated skill development.

There is a hidden benefit to this step: Every bit of new knowledge and every ounce of new mastery fuels the fire of passion. You will become more passionate about what you do and how you do it. That passion is felt by those around you, and it will add immeasurable value to your work.

exercise two

Write down two areas where you need to acquire new knowledge or skills, or polish an existing skill.

1. _____
_____
_____
_____

2. _____
_____
_____
_____

Now write this as your "bonus goal" on the lines next to number four on your Goals sheet (exercise one).

1. set goals
2. study hard
3. **seek need**
4. share expertise
5. step up
6. say thanks

It is literally true that you can
succeed best and quickest
by helping others to succeed.

- napolean hill

3. seek need

It's time to put your new knowledge to use. Your new audience is out there, in the form of people who need your skills. You just need to find them. How can you best become acquainted with those who need your newly acquired/polished skills?

Sometimes there are existing venues, like community organizations, that are ready-made for meeting your new audience. Other times you can create or purchase a list of people to whom you can offer your services.

If it is really hard to find ways to meet those in need of your knowledge, then identify people who can *introduce you* to your new audience. We can call them "gate-keepers" or "referral sources" or "influencers." Make a list of professionals who are related to your new goal, but who might not be the decision-makers you seek.

For example, if you are looking for people who want to sell their homes, you might think of who else they will talk to: financial advisors, real estate attorneys, divorce attorneys, CPAs, mortgage brokers, and contractors. Each of these folks will likely play some role in the sale of the home.

Another example is if you are looking for music promoters to help you launch your new album, you would approach their associates: other musicians they represent, attorneys, producers, booking agents, and PR specialists.

In many cases, you can meet these people at networking or industry/trade events. For some of you, the word "networking" elicited an uncontrolled eye-roll. This just means you have been doing it wrong. It's okay. Most people do it wrong. The purpose of networking *is not* to exchange names, occupations, and business cards. The true purpose *is* to personally connect with other professionals in a genuine way. When done correctly, networking is an authentic expression of interest in other people. I can't think of anything less worthy of an eye-roll.

You will likely find that each person brings something special to his/her job — in fact, that is what makes it more than a "job." That is where the magic happens. So, look for "rockstars" in each field. These are the people who are excelling and serving the audience you want to serve. Ask them to tell you about the keys to their success. You might learn something that can help you elevate your business. The research you have been doing from Step Two is creating genuine enthusiasm within you. This means that you don't need to whip up that fake smile for the event. Your new passion should bring a smile to your lips without much effort.

Step Two is also helping you build confidence. The more you take your knowledge and skill growth into your own hands, the more confidence you will exude. The most effective cure for self-doubt is education. Every book you read and class you take is an investment in your education. Warren Buffett said in a Q&A session in 2008, "The most important investment you can make is in yourself." He's nicknamed the "Oracle of Omaha," so I would listen to him.

Here's how you can network like a champ:

- Dress for success.
- Attend an event.
- Approach someone.
- Introduce yourself and allow him/her to do the same.
- Find out what makes him/her unique in his/her field.
- Decide if he/she is the kind of person you would like to get to know better. If so, exchange business cards and make a note to invite him/her to have coffee with you.
- Then, excuse yourself and move on to the next person.
- Follow up later that day or the next morning with a phone call and an invitation to join you for a cup of coffee. If you are forced to leave a voicemail message, follow up that message with an email, as well.
- During your coffee meeting, find out what his/her goals are and how you can help. An easy way to do this is by asking who his/her best prospects are. This will help you to identify relevant referrals. Now that you have a list of clear

goals and the list of resources you need, you can share with him/her what you are trying to accomplish.

Besides networking, there is another way to meet influencers. In the book "The Tipping Point," Malcolm Gladwell identified a category of people he called "connectors." They are the people who seem to know everyone and they love making introductions. You likely have some of these people in your life already. They will have suggestions of whom you should meet — they might even introduce you to them.

When you plan to meet influencers or potential referrers, be dressed in a way that communicates your professionalism. That can also be said for the rest of the time you spend in public. A chance encounter at the grocery store could lead to a life-changing opportunity. Dressing for success also has a psychological effect. Once you dress for the position you want, your mind starts to feel as though you are worthy and ready to earn it.

Sometimes there are not obvious ways to meet decision-makers, influencers, or connectors. In this rare case, your options are reduced to the more passive methods of outreach, like direct mail or advertising. Make no mistake: these are not only more expensive, but also usually less effective. The more personal your method of outreach, the better. If all you have is a name and address, and it is not appropriate to stop by for a visit, try sending a handwritten note that includes a "call to action." This can be as simple as, "I'd love to meet with you for a few minutes on Wednesday. Please let me know what time is best." This note is more likely to be read than a computer-generated letter or a mass-mailed postcard.

Michael Maher created a hierarchy of effective communication methods in his book "7 Levels of Communication." He placed advertising at the bottom and one-on-one meetings at the top. Let's face it: Advertising no longer has the power it once did. We are so inundated with multimedia marketing efforts that we have learned to tune them out. Therefore, in-person meetings are the best way to make a personal connection and a lasting impression.

I like to think of it as two general categories of outreach: Passive and active. Passive outreach is like fishing — you dangle the lure in front of a large audience of people and hope that someone is attracted to it. Active outreach is more like hunting — you find the person you want to reach and you approach him/her. Passive outreach is more expensive, less targeted, has a longer lead-time, and is less effective. Not only is active outreach more effective and faster at generating progress, but it also places the responsibility on us. We *make* progress happen; we don't wait for it.

No matter the method, begin your outreach now. Make it a priority every day. As the old saying goes, "This is where the rubber meets the road."

exercise three

Write down three ways you can meet people who need your newly acquired knowledge and ways you can meet people who can *introduce you* to your new audience.

1. _____

   _____

   _____

2. _____

   _____

   _____

3. _____

   _____

   _____

1. set goals
2. study hard
3. seek need
4. share expertise
5. step up
6. say thanks

today knowledge has power.
it controls access to opportunity
and advancement.

\- peter drucker

4. share expertise

It's time to put this new knowledge to use. Ask yourself, "What is the best way to share this knowledge with those who need it?" One of the most exciting things about the current state of technology is that it is much easier to syndicate your content; to create content once for multiple uses. Let me explain how.

Let's say you are a real estate agent and you write a brief article about five ways clients can prepare their homes for sale so that it will sell quicker and for more money. You did the research and the writing once. Here are the next steps to get the most out of it:

- Submit your article to the local newspaper or news website.
- Post it on your blog or website.
- Offer it for use to your colleagues in related businesses, like mortgage brokers or financial advisors.
- Include it in your monthly mass email to clients, friends, and colleagues.
- Use it as a letter or article in a newsletter you mail to prospects.
- Record it as a podcast.

- Record it as a video to be shared on YouTube.
- Present it in a talk to a live audience at an existing event (like the Chamber of Commerce) or in an event that you host.

There are likely additional ways your article can be used. But, by using only the methods listed above, you have already multiplied the effective use of your article by a factor of eight!

Keep in mind that the information you are sharing should be useful for your desired clientele. Avoid the "look at how great I am" style of marketing that can be annoying, unless the reason you are "great" is something that truly matters — and even then, make sure it is written to benefit the audience; not solely to benefit your ego. The best content is genuinely written for the audience.

Another benefit to writing is that you will be seen as an expert. I remember long ago hearing someone say, "Experts write." It's true. My friend, Jack Cotton, began making and distributing market reports in the early years of his real estate business. New York real estate expert and celebrity, Barbara Corcoran, did the same thing with her "Corcoran Report." By putting information on paper and sending it to those who could use it, they became known as experts. Mr. Cotton built a powerful, luxury real estate company on Cape Cod, Massachusetts. Ms. Corcoran became a world-renowned businesswoman and is often quoted by the New York Times! You can imagine what that does for her business.

If you are having trouble finding an outlet for your knowledge, use the "influencers" you know to distribute it to those in need. As I noted in the aforementioned list, colleagues in related industries are often looking for content for their own newsletters or blogs. Many of the websites out there are content-hungry. You can help them with content, while they can help you with distribution and exposure.

You can also use this content as part of your follow-up by putting it in your drip campaigns. A drip campaign is simply a series of emails sent to potential prospects.

Not everyone is a great writer. But, you have been learning a lot of great content in your studies from Step Two in this book. That means the knowledge is fresh in your mind. Lucky for you, our attention spans have been shrinking. Some of the most popular articles you can write are short lists. Think of titles that begin with, "The top five reasons you should..." or "The top three ways to...." Write the list concisely. Then, find a friend to help you edit. It doesn't need to be perfect. It just needs to be useful to your audience.

You can also use these efforts to generate opportunities. If you were a real estate agent, you could conduct interviews with recent buyers to find out "Three things people wish they knew before they bought their homes." Not only would this make tremendously useful content, but it would put you in touch with home owners. You could call or write to them and ask to interview them briefly for an article you are writing. Many people would be thrilled to be quoted in an article. You could also ask potential referrers, such as CPAs, for their advice to buyers or sellers. One article could be, "Five benefits of putting your home in a trust." Not only will you forge a relationship with your colleague and provide useful information to potential clients, but you will also add to your growing breadth of knowledge.

I cannot emphasize enough that this does not need to be complicated. It can be this simple:

- Brainstorm article topic. (30 mins)
- Create a list of interview questions. (30 mins)
- Make a list of potential interviewees and reach out to them. (60-120 mins)
- Write the article. (60 mins)
- Distribute it. (30 mins)

In just three-to-four hours, you will have written a great article that will soon establish you as an expert. And, better yet, you will have created something that will help your potential clients.

You can also use this process (with a little tweaking) to create a panel discussion for an event. As the moderator, you will be seen as an expert among experts. Select three to five experts for your panel. These can be past clients, people in related fields, local thought-leaders, politicians, etc. As an interviewer or a moderator, use your listening skills. Someone once said to me, "You were given one mouth and two ears. Use them proportionately." That is great advice.

exercise four

Write down three ways you can share your new knowledge.

1. _____

   _____

   _____

2. _____

   _____

   _____

3. _____

   _____

   _____

1. set goals
2. study hard
3. seek need
4. share expertise
5. **step up**
6. say thanks

action is the foundational key
to all success.
- pablo picasso

5. step up

Let's take a moment to review: You set goals in Step One so that you could understand where opportunities need to take you. In Step Two, you began accumulating the skills and knowledge necessary to prepare you for the opportunities to come. You discovered where to find your new audience and how to share your information with it in Steps Three and Four. Now you need to train yourself to recognize and grasp the opportunities you are creating.

Step Five is the most important step because this is where the magic happens — it's really the purpose of this entire book! I said earlier that luck is an opportunity that has been recognized and grasped. So how do we recognize it?

When someone presents you with an invitation to do something or meet someone, ask yourself the following questions...

- Will this get me closer to my goals?
- Will this allow me to practice my new (or newly polished) skills and knowledge?
- Will my contribution position me as an expert in my field?

- Will I meet people who can help me achieve my goals?
- Will I meet people who *know* people who can help me achieve my goals?

If the answer to any of these questions is "yes" or "maybe," you should accept the invitation. In the beginning, you should accept most invitations. It makes sense to start broadly and to edit later, as opposed to starting too narrowly. Remember: An opportunity doesn't need to take you all the way to your goal. It just needs to move you closer.

Here is an example: Let's say you are a newly licensed real estate agent and you were offered a rental client lead. Maybe you are trying to build a sales career, so this rental doesn't look like it will get you to your goal. But, will you be practicing your skills? Yes. Will you meet people who can help you achieve your goals? The renter might one day buy a home from you (if you do a great job and stay in touch), so the answer is yes. He/she also might have friends who would like to rent or buy. As you can see, that rental is starting to look like it could help you build your sales career.

Let's try another: Maybe you would love to secure a job at a highly competitive advertising agency, but you have been told you are not qualified. You might apply as an intern to work two or three days per week at the agency, while you do something else to pay the bills. Will you get closer to your goals? While you won't get rich as an intern, you *will* get in the door and learn the business, so the answer is yes. Will you meet people who can help you achieve your goals?

You will get to know influencers within the company, so the answer is yes. While you are there, you can also ask those you admire for suggestions to help you build your skill set. Even if it doesn't turn into your dream job, you can use that experience and your new connections to open doors elsewhere.

So what if no one has presented you with an invitation to do something or meet someone? It is time to get a little more proactive. Before your next coffee meeting or networking function, prepare a question or two that might yield a result. For instance, describe, in as much detail as possible, the kind of person who might be able to help you — whether you describe a client or a potential influencer. Ask your colleague or friend if he/she knows someone like that and if you could be introduced.

Once you have grasped the opportunity, the next step is to make the most of it. Ask yourself how you can turn this into *more* opportunities. This is a secret skill that successful people have honed. Here are some suggestions to help you create exponential opportunity:

1. Do great work. This is your chance to shine, so make it count. Be prepared. Be accountable. Be professional. Be "recommendable."
2. Look for areas where you can provide more than was asked of you. We tend to remember when a service provider did more than we expected. Exceeding expectations is one excellent way to promote yourself.

40

3. Anticipate problems and work around them. Resourcefulness, not cleanliness, is next to godliness. (But, cleanliness is good, too.)

4. Communicate clearly and often. The number one complaint that clients have about their real estate agents is that they do not communicate enough. I bet the real estate industry isn't alone in this issue.

5. Follow-up after the job or task is complete. An electrician once told me that his work had a "taillight guarantee" — it was guaranteed for as long as I could see his taillights. Don't abandon a client just because the job is done. Keep in touch.

6. Ask for honest feedback. You will learn everything you need to know (and, perhaps, more than you'd like to hear) about how you can improve your business. Be open to the feedback. Let your clients become your partners in your growth.

7. Ask if there are additional opportunities. Too often, entrepreneurs don't ask for referrals or additional business. In fact, your clients may think that if you don't ask for more work, you don't want it or don't have time for it.

8. Ask for introductions to like-minded people. If there isn't more work available from that client, tell him/her you enjoyed working with him/her and would love to work with anyone he/she likes or respects.

9. Market the accomplishment. Whether you ask the client to recommend you online or you blog about the

experience, make sure your audience knows you are actively succeeding. People only want to hire those who are successful.

Once you have gotten the opportunity flowing, your job is to keep up the momentum. Author Brian Tracy said, "I've found that luck is quite predictable. If you want more luck, take more chances. Be more active. Show up more often." That is why I call Step Five "Step Up." It is time to step up to the plate or take your seat at the table, or, as author Sheryl Sandberg says, it's time to "lean in."

You need to grab opportunities when they come. They might not take you all the way to the finish line of your goals — in fact, they *rarely* do. But, they take you closer. Treat each opportunity like the gift it is and do your best to follow it as far as it will take you. The more chances you take, the more opportunities you will see, until the world seems designed for you to succeed.

There is one last thing we need to discuss in Step Six: Obstacles. They are going to happen. The first will probably appear roughly at the time that you start to hit your stride. Something is going to get in your way. Right now you can't imagine what it will be. But, it will happen.

You need to keep going. If the obstacle is immovable, find another way to get to your goal. Think of your goal again as your destination on a map. In this case, let's say that your destination is your home after a long day of work. Each turn gets you closer. But — it's happened to me and I bet it's happened to you — you come upon a construction detour or a fallen tree branch. Do you turn around and go back to the office? Of course not! You find another route. It seems obvious when you are driving home. It needs to be just as obvious when you are working toward your goal.

There is a chance that the first obstacle will be words of discouragement coming from someone you trust, admire, or count as a friend. You might hear, "That's never going to work," or, "Don't waste your time." Thank that person for his/her concern. Then tell him/her this: "Progress has only ever been made by people who have had the sheer guts and determination to step outside of their comfort zones. Today I am that person."

There is also a chance that the obstacle may come from within, in the form of negative "self-talk" or fear. In that case, the mantra is the same. But, you say it to yourself.

exercise five

Write down opportunities as they appear. Then, underneath each one, write down two or three ways you can take it to the next level.

1. _____

    a. _____

    b. _____

    c. _____

2. _____

    a. _____

    b. _____

    c. _____

3. _____

    a. _____

    b. _____

    c. _____

4. _____

    a. _____

    b. _____

    c. _____

5. _____

    a. _____

    b. _____

    c. _____

6. _____

    a. _____

    b. _____

    c. _____

7. _____

    a. _____

    b. _____

    c. _____

8. _____

    a. _____

    b. _____

    c. _____

1. set goals
2. study hard
3. seek need
4. share expertise
5. step up
6. say thanks

take time to be kind
and to say 'thank you.'

- zig ziglar

6. say thanks

Gratitude has been a hot topic of conversation lately, particularly since it plays a leading role in recent books like Shawn Achor's "The Happiness Advantage." He suggests writing three gratitudes each morning as part of a proven program to become happier. The added bonus is that it also helps your business.

One way to assure future help is by being grateful for the help you have received. People are helping you get closer to your goals and you should acknowledge it. These people may be clients, colleagues, referrers, teachers, mentors, family, or friends. I have even written notes of gratitude to authors and philanthropists, thanking them for their generosity. I was shocked to get notes back in response — I even received a gift!

Too often good deeds go unrewarded. A simple "thank you" goes a long way. A small, thoughtful gift goes even farther. Send a handwritten note at the very least. Make it easier for yourself by having cards, envelopes and stamps somewhere handy; keep them on your desk and in your car.

There is something surprising about saying thank you: it is just as important for you as it is for the person to whom you say it. The act of showing gratitude helps your brain record a mental note about where you found the opportunity and what it looked like. This helps you recognize more opportunities in the future.

exercise 6

Write thank you notes (with gifts, if possible) for each person who gets you one step closer to your goal. Keep track below.

1. _____
2. _____
3. _____
4. _____
5. _____
6. _____
7. _____
8. _____
9. _____
10. _____
11. _____
12. _____
13. _____
14. _____
15. _____
16. _____
17. _____
18. _____

summary

As I stated in the introduction, luck is merely opportunity that has been recognized and grasped. We only need to train our minds to look for it; then train ourselves to grasp it. When we do, success is inevitable.

I hope this book is useful to you. It was certainly enjoyable to write! Contact me if you have any questions or comments about what you have read. Please share your experiences with "There Is No Such Thing As Luck" by emailing me at colleen@colleenbarry.com.

If you'd like to read more, the following is a list of helpful books that I recommend:

Regarding motivation, mindset, and the brain:
- "The Happiness Advantage" by Shawn Achor
- "Start: Punch Fear in the Face" by Jon Acuff
- "The Success Principles" by Jack Canfield
- "Mindset" by Carol Dweck
- "The Miracle Morning" by Hal Elrod
- "Leap First" by Seth Godin

- "Your Brain at Work" by David Rock

Regarding entrepreneurialism, sales, and business:
- "Lead with Luv" by Ken Blanchard and Colleen Barrett
- "Selling Luxury Homes" by Jack Cotton
- "The E Myth" by Michael Gerber
- "7 Levels of Communication" by Michael Maher
- "The Go-Giver" by Bob Burg and John David Mann
- "Goals!" by Brian Tracy

Regarding sharing the limelight:
- "Limelight Larry" by Leigh Hodgkinson: A children's book about a peacock who doesn't want to include his friends in the book he is writing so that he can hog the limelight. This was recommended (and given) to me by my wonderful friend and colleague, Kyle Kaagan, who *desperately* wanted to be in this book. You made it, Kyle.

notes

1. Matthews, Gail, Ph.D., "Goals Research", Dominican University, 2007
2. Direct Marketing Association with Bizo and Epsilon, "Response Rate Report", Direct Mail News, 2012

about the author

For more than a decade, Colleen Barry has been a proud member of the leadership team at Gibson Sotheby's International Realty. In her role as Director of Productivity, she offers group seminars and classes, as well as one-to-one coaching. She notes that humor is an integral part of the process. The firm's sales have more than tripled since 2006 (source: MLSpin, 2015). She is also a contributing writer for Inman News.

A New England native, Mrs. Barry was born and raised in Connecticut before moving to Massachusetts. She has lived in Greater Boston for nearly 20 years. In her personal time, Mrs. Barry is a good cook, a decent photographer, a mediocre guitarist, and a terrible tennis player.

Made in the USA
Middletown, DE
07 June 2015